Who Lives on the Cold, Icy Tundra?

Rachel Lynette

PowerKiDS press.

New York

To Dewayne, who will see the penguins someday, maybe even with me

Published in 2011 by The Rosen Publishing Group, Inc.
29 East 21st Street, New York, NY 10010

First Edition

Editor: Joanne Randolph
Book Design: Greg Tucker
Photo Researcher: Jessica Gerweck

Photo Credits: Cover, pp. 5, 7, 8, 10, 11, 13, 14, 15, 16, 18, 20–21, 22 Shutterstock.com; p. 4 © www.iStockphoto.com/Ryerson Clark; p. 6 Mark Lewis/Getty Images; p. 9 Paul McCormick/Getty Images; p. 12 Eastcott Momatiuk/Getty Images; p. 17 Darrell Gulin/Getty Images; p. 19 © www.iStockphoto.com/Richard Sidey.

Library of Congress Cataloging-in-Publication Data

Lynette, Rachel.
  Who lives on the cold, icy tundra / Rachel Lynette. — 1st ed.
      p. cm. — (Exploring habitats)
  Includes index.
  ISBN 978-1-4488-0675-1 (library binding) — ISBN 978-1-4488-1279-0 (pbk.) — ISBN 978-1-4488-1280-6 (6-pack)
  1. Tundra animals—Arctic regions—Juvenile literature. I. Title.
  QL105.L97 2011
  591.75'86—dc22
                                            2009054351

Manufactured in the United States of America

CPSIA Compliance Information: Batch #WS10PK: For Further Information contact Rosen Publishing, New York, New York at 1-800-237-9932

Contents

What Is the Tundra?

Unless you live very far south, very far north, or high on a mountain, you have likely never been to the tundra. Very few people live on the tundra because it is a **harsh**, cold **environment**.

There are two kinds of tundra. One kind is called alpine tundra.

Baffin Island is part of icy Nunavut. This island's land is Arctic tundra.

Alpine tundra is the land above the tree line on mountains. This land is at high **altitudes**, where the air is cold and trees cannot grow. Another kind of tundra is the Arctic tundra. The Arctic tundra runs from the North Pole through parts of Alaska, northern Canada, and Russia.

Both kinds of tundra have some things in common. Some of these common **features** are low **temperatures**, no trees, poor nutrients, short growing seasons, and fewer kinds of plants and animals than warmer places.

Tundra is not always covered in snow. However, there is always a layer of permafrost, or frozen ground, beneath the top of the soil.

It is so cold on the tundra that much of the ground stays frozen all year long. The **average** temperature in the Arctic tundra is -18° F (-28° C) but it can get as cold as -94° F (-70° C). In the summer it gets warm enough for the top of

Here it is summer on the Alaskan tundra. Rivers and pools of water form as ice and snow melt.

the soil to melt. However, because of the **permafrost** beneath this soil, trees cannot grow. Only low-growing plants with short roots, such as bushes, wildflowers, grasses, mosses, and **lichens**, can grow on the tundra.

When the top part of the soil melts, the ground can be very wet. Marshes, lakes, bogs, and streams can cover the landscape. This brings lots of bugs and birds to the Arctic tundra during the summer months.

Winter on the tundra is very cold. Polar bears are well suited to living in this climate, though.

7

Arctic Animals

Even though it is very cold and windy on the tundra, some animals can live there. However, most of these animals do not stay on the tundra all year. Instead, they **migrate** to places where it is warmer during the coldest winter months.

Here a snowy owl rests on the snow-covered tundra. Snowy owls, ptarmigan, and snow geese have layers of feathers to keep them warm.

Animals that live in the Arctic have **adapted** to the harsh weather. **Mammals** have thick layers of fur to keep them warm. Caribou have hollow hair that holds warm air near their bodies. Musk oxen have soft, woolly fur underneath their heavy, outside coats. Small mammals like Arctic hares, lemmings, and voles burrow under the snow to stay warm.

Many Arctic animals, such as grizzly bears and polar bears, have a thick layer of fat under their skin that helps keep them warm.

The Arctic Fox

Arctic foxes have thick coats that have two jobs. Their coats keep them warm in temperatures as low as -58° F (-50° C). They even have fur on the bottoms of their paws to keep their feet warm.

An arctic fox in its white winter coat moves along the tundra. It hunts for small animals using its sharp eyes and sense of smell.

Their coats also help them blend in. The coat is white in winter to blend in with the snow. In summer, the coat becomes gray or brown to match the landscape.

Arctic foxes eat lemmings, hares, voles, and other small animals.

Arctic foxes will also follow a polar bear and eat what the polar bear leaves behind. However, the foxes must be careful or they will become the polar bear's food, too!

This baby arctic fox, called a kit, comes out of its den in the summer. Do you see how its darker fur helps it blend with the rocks?

Antarctic Animals

Antarctica is even colder than the Arctic. Almost all of it is covered in ice. No land mammals live in Antarctica. However, six **species** of seals live in the sea around Antarctica.

Migrating birds, such as this giant petrel, come to Antarctica's shores. They come to eat penguin babies and eggs, among other animals.

Although they spend most of their time in the water, seals must come on land to breed, or make babies. Seals have a thick layer of fat to help them stay warm in the icy waters and on land.

When most people think of Antarctic animals, they likely think of penguins.

There are 17 species of penguins, but only 4 kinds breed on Antarctica. These are the Adélie, the emperor, the chinstrap, and the gentoo penguins.

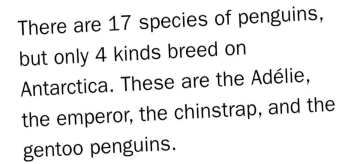

Crabeater, leopard, Ross, and elephant seals are some of the seals that live around Antarctica. Some seals form huge colonies at breeding time, but not all of them do.

Powerful Swimming Penguins

Penguins live in large groups, called rookeries. On land, penguins often huddle together to stay warm. Penguins spend most of their time in the water. Some kinds spend as much as 75 percent of their life at sea!

The biggest penguins in Antarctica are emperor penguins.

Can you guess why this penguin is called the chinstrap penguin? Chinstrap penguins lay two eggs in November or December, which hatch in February or March.

They are about 45 inches (114 cm) tall. Powerful and fast in the water, they can dive down more than 1,800 feet (550 m). They can also hold their breath for over 20 minutes.

14

Penguins have waterproof feathers and a thick layer of fat under their skin to help them live in the cold Antarctic Ocean.

One of the most common penguins in Antarctica is the Adélie penguin. There are around 2.5 million pairs. Adélie penguins are about 27.5 inches (70 cm) tall.

Emperor penguins do not build nests. Instead the male penguin holds the egg on his feet to keep it warm. He will not eat for nine weeks.

Coming and Going

Many animals come to the tundra during the spring and summer and migrate to warmer places for the cold winter. Caribou travel in large herds. There may be more than 10,000 animals in a single herd.

Arctic terns breed in the Arctic tundra during summer. Then they fly around 12,000 miles (19,312 km) to Antarctica. This trip can take months!

A herd of caribou may migrate over 500 miles (800 km) from the forests in the south to the tundra. They come to the tundra to eat lichen. They use their hooves to cut through ice and snow to find this yummy dinner.

Many birds migrate to the tundra in the warmer months, when the melting ice makes bogs. These are an excellent home for waterbirds like ducks, geese, and sandpipers. These birds stay a few months to breed and then fly south, sometimes for thousands of miles (km).

There are about five million caribou living in the Arctic and alpine tundras and northern forests around the world. Caribou are also called reindeer in some places.

Alpine Animals

The alpine tundra is home to many **grazing** animals, such as alpacas, llamas, yaks, and elks. All of these animals have thick coats to keep them warm. Some grazing animals, such as mountain goats and blue sheep,

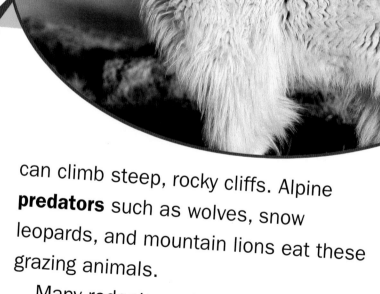

Mountain goats live in northwestern North America, from the Cascade Range and Rocky Mountains into parts of Alaska. They spend their summers in alpine meadows.

can climb steep, rocky cliffs. Alpine **predators** such as wolves, snow leopards, and mountain lions eat these grazing animals.

Many rodents and other small animals also make their homes on the alpine tundra. Marmots, snowshoe hares, ground squirrels, and voles live in **burrows**. They are always on the lookout for predators like foxes, weasels, and eagles.

Musk oxen live mainly on the Arctic tundra. They may move up into mountains during winter to find food when snow in the valleys is too deep.

Busy Pikas

Pikas are small mammals related to rabbits. Pikas eat grasses, small branches, moss, and lichen. They make their burrows in rocky areas of the alpine tundra.

This pika carries an alpine meadow plant in its mouth. Pikas are very busy during the summer months while plants are growing.

During the summer, pikas gather grasses from nearby meadows. They lay the grasses out on rocks to dry in the summer sun. They then line their burrows with this hay to keep them warm in the winter months.

Sometimes, pikas will try to steal hay from other pikas. This causes fighting. Fighting pikas need to be careful, though. Plenty of hungry alpine animals, such as ferrets and large birds, are always on the lookout for easy food.

An Icy Life

Life on the tundra is not easy. Even animals that have adapted to the weather may not live through the winter. However, if an animal dies, it is not wasted. It becomes much-needed food for other animals.

This snow leopard is hunting prey on the tundra. There are only between 3,000 and 7,000 of these animals left in the wild!

Animals that are strong enough to make it to summer are rewarded. For a few months, there is plenty of food and the chance to find a mate and breed. Then the cycle of life on the tundra continues.

Glossary

adapted (uh-DAPT-ed) Changed to fit requirements.

altitudes (AL-tuh-toodz) Heights above Earth's surface.

average (A-vrij) Usual.

burrows (BUR-ohz) Holes an animal digs in the ground for shelter.

environment (en-VY-ern-ment) All the living things and conditions of a place.

features (FEE-churz) The special look or form of a person or an object.

grazing (GRAYZ-ing) Feeding on grass.

harsh (HAHRSH) Rough or hard.

lichens (LY-kenz) Plantlike living things made of algae and fungi.

mammals (MA-mulz) Warm-blooded animals that have backbones and hair, breathe air, and feed milk to their young.

migrate (MY-grayt) To move from one place to another.

permafrost (PUR-muh-frost) A layer of soil below the surface that is always frozen.

predators (PREH-duh-terz) Animals that kill other animals for food.

species (SPEE-sheez) One kind of living thing. All people are one species.

temperatures (TEM-pruh-cherz) How hot or cold things are.

Index

Web Sites

Due to the changing nature of Internet links, PowerKids Press has developed an online list of Web sites related to the subject of this book. This site is updated regularly. Please use this link to access the list:
www.powerkidslinks.com/explore/cit/

24